journey in shades

poetry in light and dark

mary pargeter

CBP

GB Publishing.org

First published by
GBP
GB Publishing.org

Copyright ©2013 Mary Pargeter
All rights reserved
ISBN: 978-0-9572970-4-3

A catalogue record of this book
is available from the British Library

Cover design ©2013 Mary Pargeter Design
www.pargeterdesign.co.uk

GBP

GB Publishing.org
www.gbpublishing.org

With thanks to friend and fellow
writer Brenda Marsh for her constant
encouragement and lasting support

childhood

love

death

reflection

childhood

duntroon

After the war we bought Duntroon.
My mother said the Persian carpets
Crumbled in your hands.
A working house now
For our market garden.
Scullery for Wellingtons,
Raeburn for cooking,
Tin bath before its warmed towels.
Galleried hall for roller skating,
Servants bells on back stairs, long unused,
Library with french doors to downs view,
Study with worn leather chair,
Box rooms for trunks and chests,
Bedrooms of different colours,
Bathroom with plans for henhouse,
Corridors, steps up, steps down,
Drawing room with shuttered sashes
And sofas for jumping.
Lean-to glasshouse with
Old stove and grapevine.
Outside, the Morris,
Unmoved and rotting,
Narrow-laned tomato houses,
Rows of stems neatly tied,
Hot, humid, heavy with aroma.
Our yew tree house with
Its child-size entrance,
The field of long grass
For hiding and crawling,
Swimming pool, scratchy with
Hand-applied concrete.
And Sally, our playmate,
Barking and jumping as the
Gun's taken down for rabbit shooting.

running board ride

Scruffy and windblown, I see us now
The summer sun beating down
On the winding lane
Up to our hilltop house,
Hanging from running boards,
As the car, stately and lamp-winged,
Pulls away, chased by our frantic dog.
Past spreading corn fields,
Farms and stables, dry, dusty and
Silent in the hot afternoon.
Past the stone gates
Topped with carved pineapples
Into the shade of chalk banks
Where celandines grow
And beech tree roots entwine
Above badger and rabbit hollows.
Still up and up
To the scattering of cottages
And into the courtyard, where
Potatoes are weighed,
Sheets twisted,
Chickens' necks wrung
And feathers plucked.
And where I hide from strangers
Behind a mother's skirts.

soft dust

Warm hens' eggs hanging in hessian sacks
As small fingers feel for
Smoothness in the straw.
Lovely, lovely the dust and dark of
Our old stables and henhouse,
Delicious the smell of age and neglect.
Underfoot, decades of compacted
Soft dust and desiccated straw,
Springy but firm.
Clambering up, across beams
To our dirty dark loft house,
Boxes arranged for storymaking.
Then bright out onto the lead walkway
Between slate pitched roofs
And the dared jump to the road.

near a girl

My slender mother
As near to a girl
As I remember you,
Sitting before a
Dressing table mirror
In a light dressing gown,
Your long black hair
Brushed by the virgin hands
Of your maiden aunt,
Orphan and spinster
Paired by tragedy.
War killing her lover,
Childbirth killing your mother,
Father leaving forever.
I watch in the bedroom
Full of mahogany
In the airy, cool hush of
A country afternoon.
Your husband back from
The war, prison camp and
His own personal hell
Violating your gentility.

chalk lane to school

Down, down the chalk path
Beating nettles with sticks,
Wildflowers mixed under hazel bows
In the dappled shade.
Early morning sun on the dry chalk downs,
We village children walk to school,
A diamond paned, flint school, the
Playing field edged with an
Arched-top wall of lichen brick.
And opposite, in grandeur on the
Sloping hill, Rotherfield House and
The magnificent Hampshire trees.
And after school, when it rains,
Next door in the blacksmith's forge,
We wait, watching red coals flare,
As Gip Moss shoes a horse
To the clang of hammer
And the smell of coal and iron.

teapot memory

Green teapot
Delicate with gold ornament
On the schoolroom table
In this airy hall of learning.
Below a tall sash window
And there the misty outline of a pupil
Within ordered rows of desks,
The shadow memory of a
Woman now old or dead.
I am too young for school,
Younger even than the children
My mother is teaching to read, her
Grey outline moving silently before
The ranks of sloping desks.
At lunch, the long-remembered
Shadow of her, seated at the
Teacher's table, a cream tin of
Paste sandwiches, and most
Vivid, the green teapot
Delicate with gold ornament.

the tallboy's drawer

Why are you crying
My gentle mum,
Standing before the open drawer
With your silky hair
Wrapped around
A thin black ribbon?
I stare across the galleried landing.
I am very small here
Rooted on my little matchstick legs.
Simple and white as linen
Against the dark wood,
While your slim, bowed figure
Sears into my child's mind.
This matters. Like my
Helter-skelter terror,
Or abandonment on the
Merry-go-round among the
Fixed stares of prancing horses,
Or the sea surface lapping
As I am carried, chest high
By a father in knitted maroon trunks.
Hardwired into memory
And sometimes re-run.
Serious and still I watch.
Turning, you cover your tears
In the controlled burning
Of your mother's love.
Not yet please, her loss of innocence
But why, why were you crying
My gentle mum?

love

focus

people drift into view
linger, then fade out of focus.
you are sharp and clear
in my vision.
your teeth whiter
your laugh louder
your hair shinier
your body suppler
your voice clearer
your eyes brighter
your ears redder
your hands browner
your socks woolier
your eyebrows hairier
your clothes crisper
your tie better
so much closer
how much deeper.

tenth of november

I count the days till your return
I count again
I cross off yesterday
And count the crosses.
I write today's diary entry
Read again all the days
Since you left.
Count them, compare them,
Retrace them, study them.
Read all the entries when you were home.

Then I think of seeing you
Of how it'll be.
I imagine me running and crying.
I imagine me laughing and skipping
And squeaking and jumping
And hugging and tugging and tripping.
I imagine me smiling and kissing.
I imagine me looking and seeing your loving.
And speaking of missing your loving.
I imagine our being together
And loving.

no remembered words

We found a field.
Barley, ripe and harvest-ready
Swayed in heavy tresses,
Golden and lapping,
Far up to the curve of the hill.
An old barn stood, black and boarded.
We fell laughing into the grass.
Side by side we lay and pulled
Soft stalks. Sun-split blades
Picked by young fingers.
Like children still.
Heavy summer burned across
The valley's sweep
Woods in full leaf
Spilling over old fences, far off.
Later we moved into the barn
Climbing firm bales to our high room,
Shafts of dusty light piercing
Dark halls of space.
As I lie by your shadow
Like pale ghosts I see us now.
No remembered words or touch or look
But the smear of stickiness and
Sharp straw.

loch awe

Loch Awe lay silent
Stretching its early morning surface
Like black glass
Flat beneath a vast sky,
The forest firs
A dark diminished fringe.
Naked we ran in, hands high,
Gasping with each immersing step
At its ice coldness.
With every stroke
Black water, slapping lips,
Heaved in masses.
Lazy swells snatching breath
In fear of its depth.

We were happy then
And laughed easily,
Still young enough to play.
Believing love was easy
And simply our due,
Carelessly running forward
Unwary of its price.
But like our small, white,
Chattering bodies
We hung precarious over
Menacing shadows,
Yet to be burned by the
Slumbering scorch of pain
From its outcome.
A cost paid in full
Far down the road from Loch Awe.

loch awe still

Towelling the sparkling drops
From your olive burnished skin
You stand, my laughing young god,
Upon a lakeside rock
The sky behind
Shining across the years.
Like the dreams which come
Winging from buried memory
Spiking sleep with bittersweet calling.

once and only

I lie awake, a girl lit by
Dreams of our wedding day.
A tiny childhood bedroom
Electric with the thrill of imaginings.
I do not know yet that
Real pain will visit soon.
But now, first and last, once and only
Scenes sparkle and all is possible.
A small space of expectation
Before stark consequences
Are played out on your
Higher moral ground.
He listens and dread dawns
That he cannot condone.
He does not rant
Neither does he soften
The power of silence
Devastating dreams.

you could leave

You could leave if you promised
not a trace of you would remain
but my mind is weak with
your barren love
and I should be destroyed.

winter daffodils

You brought daffodils.
Too late.
The yellow dazzle
Innocent and cheerful,
Powerless against the corruption
Of our broken dreams.
Stricken, you held them,
Felled by my infidelity,
The consequence of
Unreciprocated love.

Letters came, full of
Penitence and promises,
Too late.
Dark nights you waited
For my return.
Once quick to leave,
Reluctant to share intimacy,
You spread out dreams.
Too late.
I hold the tattered letters,
Remorse and commitment
Like ashes in my hands.

I loved too much
For a sparse return.
Infatuation, nature's crazy magnet,
And coincidence combined
For fate's purpose,
Transient, like your despair,
And fatally destined to fail.
Diminishing back to disinterest,
You turned to new loves
And marriage.

Daffodils don't remind me,
But sometimes I remember their
Yellow brightness in your hands,
The tilt of your head
And look of anguish that
Faded, like the flowers
You held for that brief moment
When you offered dreams,
Too late.

your dark doorway

The front door stands open
As if ready for my arrival,
Planned by providence.
The devil has set his stage,
Called his actors to the table.
Motionless you sit, head bowed.
Hearing my car, you know I will pass
Through your dark doorway
From sunlight to darkness,
Hope to desolation and
The cut of betrayal.
Half smiling, unsure faces
Look across the gulf of understanding.
Familiar faces with the
Girl you will one day marry.
I stand frozen in an indelible picture
For the passing of a moment,
Then spin and stride from darkness
Into a dazzle of light,
Words dead on my lips.
Following, you lean at my window
'You shouldn't have come.'
A barely audible phrase,
Beneath it your unchangeable
Lovelessness and the
Deadly candour of ending.

Quietly spoken words,
Falling in delicate softness,
Striking against a harsh wall
As the world stands still.
Eyes fixed as stone, silent as death,
I fumble to escape, driving away
Through turmoil as the flood overwhelms.
At last we are finished.

the morning suit

I remember your wedding day.
Devil at work, at play.
Ring, ring. Call to game.
Trill, early warning in the
Pale morning light.
And a familiar voice
Complaining how
Thoughtless the driver,
Late for arrival at church.
Uncomprehending words,
Words that wound and scar,
Caustic as acid on flesh.
Let me leave, not see a soul
Dressed for a wedding.
I wander the town alone,
The slope of grey slabbed
Pavement bare as
You take your vows,
Friends and family
In celebration.
Dark, late, day done.
Open door to devil's fun.
Strewn, strewn on the armchair
Like a drunken dancer
Lay the morning suit.
Black, black and abandoned.
Flagrant, taunting display
Stark in my home,
Trampling roughshod
Over fragile feelings.
I remember the day.

clouded memory

I think of you
and clouded memories return.
I catch the sudden sensation
of your closeness
for a brief moment,
and it is gone.
I am left a void.
you look at me from afar
as my memory looks for you.

dream series

You came into my dreams last night
I looked beautiful.
I wasn't me, I was Grace Kelly
In a black mink with a white silk shirt.
I tempted you to stay
Pressing my lovely face to yours.
I think I had you then,
But interest slips to indifference
And my hold weakens.

You came into my dreams last night
Serious to make a home,
Enfolding me in unfamiliar security.
'When we are married' you say.
Words I repeat to myself
In a rose-tinted peace.

You came into my dreams last night
Across a dance floor, laughing,
Dressed in dinner suit.
Casually, someone passed your message.
Not to think you might be interested,
That you had a new girl, a double ten.

You came into my dreams last night
Talking through the window
Of a silver estate.
Climbing into the passenger seat
She put her hand on your knee.
I watched the intimacy of the interior
While a bolt struck, enough to wake.

death

the hospital room

I look across the final room
Of suffering. My mother's
Gaunt death profile in silhouette
Against a grey sky window.
Her patient sacrifice
Of painful years frozen.
Now the long weeks of struggle silenced
In that quiet, brave journey,
Never crossing the threshold
Of the secret of how it is to die.
And with your going so ends
That unconditional love.
My selfish terms deserving less.
No more words now.
One last look, one image sealed.
Goodbye the face
That smiled in welcome
I rushed and hardly stopped to see.
No more the gentle voice that
Would so love a kind reply.
Now life starts to bite
As I open doors to empty rooms,
Rooms as dead as the dear
Hands that created my lost home
Lying stilled beneath the
Draped sheet.

'not like me, mary'

Is this how I shall die?
Like my childless aunt
Alone, tended by strange hands.
By an empty bedside chair.
Obediently,
Dying dutifully,
With no fuss
As the afternoon light dims.

Is this how it ends?
The criss-cross pattern
Of a lifetime's journeys
On one detailed spot.
A sparse deathbed
A glass, a downturned sheet, an arced light.
A chair vacant with the unborn
As the afternoon light dims.

I travelled after the storm.
'You came' she breathed
Knowing death was close,
That I could stay.
Hopeful, pitiful
Her last oblique request.
Fool, I left, I left, not hearing
The death knell sounding
In her sigh of
Final resignation.
Walking from the echoing ward
As the afternoon light dimmed.

Q6 C10

I went back years
After the burial.
The cemetery staff
Looked up his
Final resting place.
Q6 C10.
Take 6 paces to R
And 10 to D.
I stared at the grass spot,
Remembering.
The sun shone on the bright grass
And my freedom.
My freedom and my curse,
The curse of isolation
Bequeathed by your destructive rule.
The fear you struck, you spun
You bind us. You wrapped us in.
The light gleams on the river.
Light beams that glint from
Ash leaves. Sharp against the grave.
Spade on stone, rasp on rasp.
Q6 C10. Fast and smart.
No epitaph this.
Let me remember the glade,
The grass, the streaming sun.
No, not that passage. Not there.
I choose lightness of spirit
And confidence.
But no, marred it must be,
Corrupted and defiled
From the outset.

not the time for dying

Now is not the time for dying
While the sun burns the land stiff and dry
And the gauzy haze of heat blinds
In the mid-afternoon glare.
It is for grass between toes
And the lip of a straw hat,
Not monitoring and measuring
And the cage of a deathbed.
Not for the dark tunnel ahead
And the aching poignancy of
Plans never fulfilled.
It is for the horizon of sea
And the seeing and sensing.

Your golden hair glowed in its prime
As you walked down the dark street
To the village dance.
A path of light that shone and swung
In a heavy blaze of gold.
Cruel, the ravaging hand of the destroyer
To take your crowning glory.

We sit together, you and I, talking
Of how beautiful are your last dawns,
Pheasants at the door, deer in the mist.
The borrowed hours diminishing.
Waiting, filling time. Speaking quietly
Of acceptance, of contentment with your life.

Listening, I watch as grazing cows,
Stark black and white in the evening sunlight,
Intermingle with the memory of the
Golden waves of your girlhood,
Colours vibrating against the
Spring green of the flood plain.

Inscrutable brown eyes that
Looked direct and enquiring
As you spoke with calm courage,
Now hold me from propped pillows.
Soft, slow, steady, as the pills sit
Unswallowed between weak lips.
You said you did not fear death,
For still dormant was the
Remorseless grip of its savagery.
Now you wake distressed, calling, struggling
To escape the bed you will never leave.
Brave you were, not deserving this horror.
You are too young to be drawn
Confused and unwilling to the grave.

But now peace has fallen
Like the drape of soft muslin.
Silent and still you lie
Beyond all understanding.
I talk but no answer now,
Words staccato in the emptiness.
You are not here. Dead as dead.
But the wisdom quietly echoes.

goodbye rob

Goodbye Rob,
You handsome devil
You wisecracker
You charmer.

Cheers Rob,
You Burgundy, Barolo, Bollinger,
Chardonnay, Chablis, Courvoisier,
Dubonnet, Drambuie, draught,
Sandemans Sherry. Shaker,
Stirrer, pourer and drinker.
'Top-up anyone?'

Bye Rob,
You natty dresser
You Prince of Wales,
Three piece check
Suited smarmer.
You pencil-thin tash
30s smoothie.

So long Rob,
The ladies loved you
Turn on the charm
With a witty line.
'Hello blue eyes'
Well, hello.
You romantic
You misogynist
You lover of women.

Cheerio Rob,
You melancholy depressive
You despondent
You politician basher
You cynic
You chooser of drinks
You filler of glasses
And dreamer to love songs.

Farewell Rob,
To the laughs, the drinks,
The boozers, the eccentrics,
The late night sleepovers
The early morning hangovers,
For tea at Kennards
And 'G&T, darling'
On your lips.

at the wake

It's like you've just walked out of the room.
A gin and tonic standing on the mantlepiece
Next to your photo in the grey suit,
The one you wore to your funeral,
And raising a glass to the camera.
Where are you now? Are you here?
If not let me tell you
It was a perfect send off.
Your wicker coffin was so pretty
With its ivy and white roses, like a
Delicate piece of country in the black hearse,
Like Spring in the bitter cold.
Did you hear the music?
Sigh to your favourites?
The vicar, humour in her smile,
Charting a chequered past, the
Poem that pulled no punches,
Hymns with taped voices,
Hardly sung any more.
Can you see us at your wake?
You outlived all but your stalwart wife,
Sat by the coal fire in a furry hat.
No old drinking partners,
No shared stories of past antics,
No tales we can only imagine,
But our generation, the next in line.

The landlord from your local did us proud.
Lovely spread and an open bar.
Of course.
It was always like that with your bashes.
You would have enjoyed it.
I don't know where you are Rob.
The gin and tonic is still waiting
Untouched. We left it in the pub
Still on the mantlepiece.

reflection

I have not always been kind

Ashamed to inflict
Your first deep wound,
I hope you do not
Think of me.
Best, not at all.
And if you remember
It is without bitterness.
You were too easy
And I too troubled
Not to hurt.
You did not deserve
My careless cruelty.
'Love, Mary, love'
Even spirits were
Moved to talk.
I have not always been kind
Or faultless or
Quick to forgive.
I hope you found love,
Are father to children,
Long-term lover to wife.
I hope you found happiness
With better than me.

distant memory

I smile softly at
Young couples in love.
Softly, in remembrance.
Their gentle gazes,
Yielding and sensuous,
Echo only for each other,
Oblivious to my wonder.
Once I soared in that
Rare place.
Sometimes a lingering smile
From the dark scene beyond
Pierced that privileged space.
An unknown sentiment,
Lightly passed over
In innocence.
Perhaps they smiled
For their own memories
As I do now for mine.

brief attraction

I sit by your side
In borderline control
Against the intensity.
Electricity pulsating,
Shots and spurs
Jumping and jarring my mind,
Jamming its pathways,
Numbing my brain,
Making me inarticulate
And imbecilic.

I have been here before.
Danger lies in those
Electric blue eyes and the
Smile that lights an unremarkable face.
Four days since and I drift
In a swooning state of
Endurance, knowing it
A matter of time to recovery.

Tonight I walk into the summer's night
And see distant stars
Measured in light years
And wonder at the mystery,
A new moon tipped on the horizon
Behind the yew tree's silhouette
As a cow calls for its young.

when the wind blows

When the wind blows
In high branches
And the rooks caw,
I am that village girl again
Who lives on the
Windswept hill,
Looking far up to the
Swirling treetops
Against a grey sky, the
Patchwork of fields beyond
Dipping to the valley floor,
Running with village children
In infinite freedom.

And when the drenching rain
Fills the courtyard to a lake,
I am that country girl crouched
In the scullery doorway
Watching half-domed bubbles
Glide slowly across the
Seething puddles.

And sometimes as the day closes
I am that little wild girl
Who cries while soft towels
Warmed by the kitchen stove
Are pressed against
Wind-battered ears.

a country childhood

I went back to the little wood
Where we swung on vines
Across the hollowed dell.
Improbable thick, hanging cords
Held a child's weight.
And there still, fist thick.
And as I clambered up the
Steep sides, the wild garlic
Pungent as ever when disturbed,
Gloss green and slippery.
We ran far from home then
Like centuries of children
Through avenues of beeches,
Spinney and copse, climbing trees.
The country imprinting like
Ink in our veins, the stain of
Blackberries and red-berried yews.

little feet

Little feet neat in shoes and socks
Above the aisle's iron grating.
Little feet suspended
Above the dark space below.
Sombre light on the patina of tiles,
Church shadows of mystery and ritual.

Graveyard tones of green,
Dark green shadow and lighter.
I wait beneath a yew while my
Mother trims the mounded grave,
Emerald green and clipped,
Of someone too aged
For me to have known.

Sometimes now I visit my
Mother's grave, quite far, and
Pull at stray grasses
Around the corroded nameplate.
Sit on the bequeathed seat
With its brass plaque,
'In Quietness and Confidence
Shall be Your Strength'
And wonder at its meaning.
It seems so long since she was here.

I have not been virtuous and
Suffered for that.
And so I take my bruises and
Shaky faith back to church
To search for peace,
Look down at the iron grating
And remember my little feet
Suspended, and their
Journey back here.

echoes among the stone arches

In the vaulted chambers
Where great men
Lie sombrely lit in
Marbled darkness,
You with your grandchildren.
History resonating
Among the stone arches
Of the crypt.
Stories half-buried
Like the bones
Beneath the service and
Awkward half-smiles.
It pains me still.
The lace christening gown, the
Remembered touch of its
Coarse pattern, lying
In a camphor drawer,
Hangs in a sweep
From a newly christened life.
Old lace and antique stone,
Disturbing textures of
Sorrowful beauty.

English poet Mary Pargeter was born in 1948 at the family home in Newton Valence, a tiny hamlet in Hampshire. Her idyllic childhood was spent running free in the exquisite landscapes near Selborne, immortalised by the 18th Century naturalist and ornithologist Gilbert White FRS.

That evocative landscape, now part of the South Downs National Park, is still referred to as Gilbert White country. In a different way, it will also always belong to Mary.

Her father had spent four years in a Japanese prisoner of war camp and her mother was a primary school teacher at the local school.

When the family moved to Surrey in 1956, to the child's dismay trees and greenery were replaced by streetlamps and pavements.

In her early 20s both parents died. A true 'child of the 60s', Mary then studied art and became a successful graphic designer. She neither married nor had children.